Beyond the Box

Beyond the Box

Dimensions of seeing
in photographs and words

Michael Frimer

GRANVILLE
ISLAND
PUBLISHING

Copyright © 2021 Linda Frimer

All rights reserved. No part of this publication may be reproduced, stored in a retrieval system or transmitted, in any form or by any means, without prior permission of the publisher or, in the case of photocopying or other reprographic copying, a license from Access Copyright, the Canadian Copyright Licensing Agency, www.accesscopyright.ca, 1-800-893-5777, info@accesscopyright.ca.

Publisher's Cataloging-in-Publication data

Names: Frimer, Michael, author.
Title: Beyond the box : dimensions of seeing in photographs and words / Michael Frimer.
Description: Vancouver, BC Canada: Granville Island Publishing, 2021.
Identifiers: ISBN: 9781989467350 (Hardcover) | 9781989467336 (pbk.)
Subjects: LCSH Frimer, Michael. | Photography, Artistic. | Conduct of life. | Art and photography. | Physicians—Biography. | BISAC PHOTOGRAPHY / Individual Photographers / Artists' Books | PHOTOGRAPHY / Photoessays & Documentaries | SELF HELP / Personal Growth / General
Classification: LCC TR655 .F75 2021 | DDC 779—dc23

Book Design: Paul DuVernet, Mica Design
Copy Editor: Marianne Ward
Cover Image: Through the Falls

Granville Island Publishing Ltd.
212–1656 Duranleau St. Granville Island
Vancouver, BC, Canada V6H 3S4

604-688-0320 / 1-877-688-0320
info@granvilleislandpublishing.com
www.granvilleislandpublishing.com

Printed in Canada on recycled paper.

To Linda

Contents

Acknowledgements	IX	Challenge Yourself	68
Foreword	X	Expectation	70
Introduction	1	Stuck	72
The Box	6	The Path to Wisdom	75
Framing Your Perspective	11	White Light	79
Between the Links	15	Text to Saudi Patient	80
Skin Deep	17	Freedom	82
Our Experience of Time	18	Communication	84
The Child is Father of the Man	27	Have a Nice Day	86
Grover's Birthday Speech	32	Sherlock Holmes	87
How Less Can Be More	35	Opposites Attract	91
What Goes Around Comes Around	38	The Ring	92
Satisfaction	40	Imagine	94
The Art of Life	41	Bring the Past Forward	101
Lessons from Nature	45	Dimensions of Silence	103
Respecting Animals	46	The Value of Leisure	106
Mistakes	51	Regeneration	110
Protection	54	Turning Out the Light	112
Appreciation	55	Celebration of Life	117
Seeking Repair	56	The Meaning of Life	120
Ripple Effect	61	At Peace	125
A Double-Edged Sword	63	Look Beyond	127
Being Humble	64	Afterword	132
Sandcastles	66	Biography	136

Under the Bridge

Acknowledgements

It is with gratitude that I thank the following people for their support in helping to bring this project to fruition.

First and foremost, I must thank my loving family, beginning with my wife, Linda, who shepherded this project through all phases of its existence. It was with her on our creative journeys that I first shared my philosophical ideas and the wonder of existence, while she always honoured and supported the artistry of my photographs.

I am thankful too for my first wife, Vicki, for her early influence and support during our wonderful years together.

Thank you to all our amazing children and their partners — Michael, Lisa, Jack, Fiorella, Aaron, Jeremy, Shoshana, Neil, Hershel, Crystal, Rachel, David, Leora and Greg, and my beautiful grandchildren Allegra, Jake, Sienna, Zava, Lev, Rafael, Jonah, Noah, Gabriel, Aliya and Elliot — for whom these thoughts were written. They have all endlessly continued, since their childhood, to be our teachers, and it is my great hope that they will always remain one strong, united family.

I also give heartfelt gratitude to my siblings and their spouses, David and Mindy, Resa and Marshall, and my sister-in-law Karen. I truly appreciate their ongoing closeness and support.

I am fortunate to have had many sources of inspiration throughout my life, beginning with Mr. Colgrove at Forest Hill Collegiate, who was the first to open up my ways of seeing, and continuing with so many beloved and life-enriching friends and colleagues. Thank you to Alex Magil and Dan Fox, both very good friends and outstanding photographers. And to my remarkable fellow surgeons, Scott Bloom, Sharad Sandpath and Marty Fishman. Thank you for ennobling my life and work.

My many thanks to Jo Blackmore and her team at Granville Island Publishing for their insight, suggestions and support with this new endeavour. I must thank wordsmiths Jessica Kaplan, Gordon Thomas, Aislinn Cottell and Marianne Ward. And many thanks to designer Paul DuVernet for his beautiful design and careful dedication to the integrity of my photographs.

Foreword

The reason Michael asked me to comment on his work was that he knew that I, too, had experienced this same geometry teacher, R.G. Pete Colgrove, and was affected by his presentations regarding the fourth dimension. It was only recently that we learned that our high school teacher had been a disciple of George Gurdjieff, a mystic and spiritual teacher who had proposed a method to awaken one's consciousness, "The Fourth Way," in order to achieve fuller personal potential. But what were we seventeen-year-olds to make of all this? These writings and photographs tell us a great deal about the impressions left by these ideas and how they played out through Michael's life.

When I first met Michael he was always accompanied by his box camera. In his text, he states that it was through the lens that he could best capture his inner feelings and beliefs. And his sense of the mystery of it all is suggested by the black and white and sometimes blurred images, always tempered by shades of grey.

Having been a vigorous and dedicated surgeon well into his seventies (and never saying he was too old), Michael finally retired due to illness. For many years these insights had guided him in the tireless care of his patients, and they may have helped him to deal with his altered situation.

He has presented us with this record so as to share his insights and excitement with family and friends. Highlights from among the many: honour the wisdom of our children; appreciate the creative power of hobbies; and accept the inconclusive perspectives of the lines that never meet.

I invite you to join me on this journey that Michael has carefully prepared for us.

– Gershon (Jerry) Growe

Jerry Growe is a retired hematologist who has practiced for forty-five years at Vancouver General Hospital and at Canadian Blood Services.

Photo by Linda Frimer

Introduction

I can still remember sitting in my high school classroom at Forest Hill Collegiate in Toronto, more than fifty years ago. Our mathematics teacher, Mr. Colgrove, was an intellectual with a particular interest in the concept of the fourth spatial dimension. One day, he asked us to look up at the classroom ceiling where it met the walls and reflect on what we saw.

We all thought this was a wild request, but we were always made curious by this remarkable teacher's intriguing ideas. He then asked us to imagine a dot. That dot would define a single location in space and therefore have no dimension.

If one added a second dot, he explained, and drew a line between the two, then anything existing on that line would be in a one-dimensional world. One-dimensional 'objects' in this world would be flat and only able to travel back and forth between the two points, along the connecting line.

If one drew another line at right angles to the first, Mr. Colgrove went on, the realm of the dots would be elevated to a second dimension, and everything from their perspective would have length and width. The dot could move anywhere in the plane, but it would still be a completely flat world.

However, if yet another line was placed at right angles to the first two, pointing 'upward', we miraculously enter the third dimension — the one we believe we are in now. A being that lived in the two-dimensional, flat-plane world would be completely unaware of this other dimension and of anything or anyone that existed within it.

Mr. Colgrove suggested that to define a fourth dimension, one would have to draw another line at right angles to each of the other three. This was what he wanted us to imagine when contemplating the corner meeting of the ceiling and walls — where would the fourth line go? The room fell silent.

Just as a being in a two-dimensional plane is unaware of a third dimension, a being in this fourth-dimensional world would be able to observe our world without us ever being aware of its existence.

I've reflected on his remarks repeatedly over the years — on the notion that there may be more to existence than we could ever realize at first glance. I was reminded yet again of my fascination with this concept when my four-year-old grandson was recently asked if he was going to visit superheroes on his upcoming trip to Disneyland. "Do they really exist?" he quizzically replied.

We define our understanding of the world on the basis of our perceptions and consciousness within it. This world is generally viewed in three dimensions, the proof of which comes to us by way of our physical experiences. The idea of a fourth dimension seems at first impossible to imagine — what direction could one go other than forward, backward; left, right; up, down?

Yet, another line does exist, and this is represented by time. We 'travel' down this dimension and can remember the journey, enabling us to perceive events with much more clarity and intensity than if we were only aware of the physical now. This awareness of time gives us a sense of the spiritual and other realms, as we question what might happen when we 'travel' into the future.

There may very well be even more dimensions yet to realize.

I recently discovered a copy of my high school yearbook that contained a poem I wrote when I was seventeen.

Question

All things are said a purpose to possess:
The youthful buds, whose blossoms dress
The otherwise bare and fruitless limb;
The holy psalm, the sacred hymn —
The drop, the pour, the river swift,
The husky boar whose meat's the gift
To fill our plates with tasty roast —
They all to have intent do boast.
And yet there's form we can't define;
The question rests: for what is man?

About twenty years ago, while in my fifties, I began writing down ideas and questions that occurred to me in my quest for a greater understanding of that which had often appeared elusive. My hope was to gather them up, check them over, and create a book that would one day leave a legacy of my life and stimulate further thoughts about at least some of the obscurities I'd encountered and grappled with.

As the saying goes, time flies, and before I knew it old age was upon me. The bits and pieces of paper on which I wrote my questions about life kept accumulating in my drawer.

In November 2018 everything changed. For several months I had noticed a difference in my memory, and prior to a planned trip to Europe, I had some blood tests that suggested I was in significant kidney failure. Assured that I could travel, it was upon immediate return from our trip, with our coats still on, that I received the

diagnosis of multiple myeloma and my world essentially fell apart.

An EEG was done, which also revealed temporal lobe epilepsy, presumably the cause of my memory loss. I would need to retire from surgical practice, after more than fifty years. I found this to be a difficult and painful experience.

Although treatment options continue to be researched, multiple myeloma remains an incurable condition. For the first time, I confronted the reality that we all ultimately face — my mortality. I came to recognize that my time on this earth was limited.

Some of the questions that I had raised over the years began to take on a new and more poignant urgency. Though the answers to almost all of them still eluded me, I knew that the questions, just by being raised, were offering potentially invaluable insight while continuously nurturing my curiosity about life's mysteries.

I've always had a strong interest in photography and have spent many hours in the darkroom throughout my life. Over time, I began to realize that many of my images captured moments of my ongoing search for understanding, viewed through focused layers of seeing, inspired by Mr. Colgrove. By reaching into the dimensions on the other side of my lens, my photography brought the intimate details surrounding me into clearer focus. This led to greater understanding — even without my camera.

So now that I'm dealing with multiple diseases that can each be defeating, I hope to spend my time within this unknown and unfamiliar darkness by recognizing it in degrees of light that has much to teach me. I hope I learn to take one step after another forward, into a gentler yet more assured sense of enlightenment.

"Someone I loved gave me a box full of darkness. It took me years to understand that this too was a gift."
– Mary Oliver

Lines Holding

The Box

Imagine three people sitting around the table, each considering what they believe might be inside the box.

The first person says it is empty, as there is no evidence of anything within.

The second heard from several others that there are chains in the box and so believes this to be so.

The third pleads ignorance and says they don't know if there is anything in the box at all, and if there is, they have no idea what it might be.

Just like there are four known dimensions, there are yet other ways of thinking. One could imagine what this box might contain: a collection of living butterflies, a heart made of Jell-O, a ball of clay, a pond of living organisms or even another realm.

The same can be said about many of our human beliefs, including the one of there being a creator or supreme force ('God') that formed and now sustains the universe. Is there a way of proving one way or another whether this entity, conceptualized by sacred or secular beliefs, exists?

Just as there can be no proof at this time as to the existence of God, until the box can be opened, we will never know whether it contains chains, something else, or if it may be empty. Perhaps all answers are valid.

The seeking of answers has often involved the creation of myths. In addition to enabling us to imbue our life with greater understanding and purpose, these myths also help us find greater comfort on our journey within creation.

The box may never be opened.

Or someone, someday, might open the mysterious box and reveal its contents. Until then, it might be wise to strive for the acquisition of knowledge and investigate life with integrity, until 'the truth' be revealed.

What's in the Box?

7

Reflecting

All Possibilities

Grid Patterning

Framing Your Perspective

From the moment we are born, society places us in a box. This creates expectations for us to live up to and boundaries for us to exist within. One such expectation is that an elderly person is frail.

Becoming an elder myself, when I saw others diminished or mistreated, I grew stronger in my convictions. I didn't want to live at this time in my life not being seen or understood for who I was or what my capabilities were. I came to trust my inner thoughts as I spent more time watching the ways people interacted with each other.

This intensified examination felt natural; it heightened my sensations much like when I viewed reality through the lens of my camera, savouring each captured moment in time. Every photo taken was the acknowledgement of an experience, a revelation of the character of someone or something.

I am hopeful that by photographing aspects of objects and people as I view them, I may also reveal something real to others — something that might lead them to think more about the imposed boundaries of their own box, the boxes of others and then what exists beyond them.

I decided to try, while facing my reality with honesty, to maintain my own perspective and follow after it as it changed. I would add play as part of my new profession called 'retirement' and do this with the complete engagement I had given to my work as a surgeon.

No matter how grey or dilapidated your outer box may appear to others, maintaining an innocent and playful sense of self throughout your life will keep you vital.

Several years ago, an elderly, retired man in his seventies went to the New York YMCA to play at the chess club. Unfortunately, the game was cancelled that day.

There just so happened to be a painting class held at the same time, and as he was about to leave the building, one of the painters asked the man to join them. He refused at first — he had never painted in his life and didn't feel very interested. Yet, eventually, he was convinced.

On a recent visit to New York, my wife, Linda, and I came across a calendar this man had painted when he was 104 years old. By this time, he had become

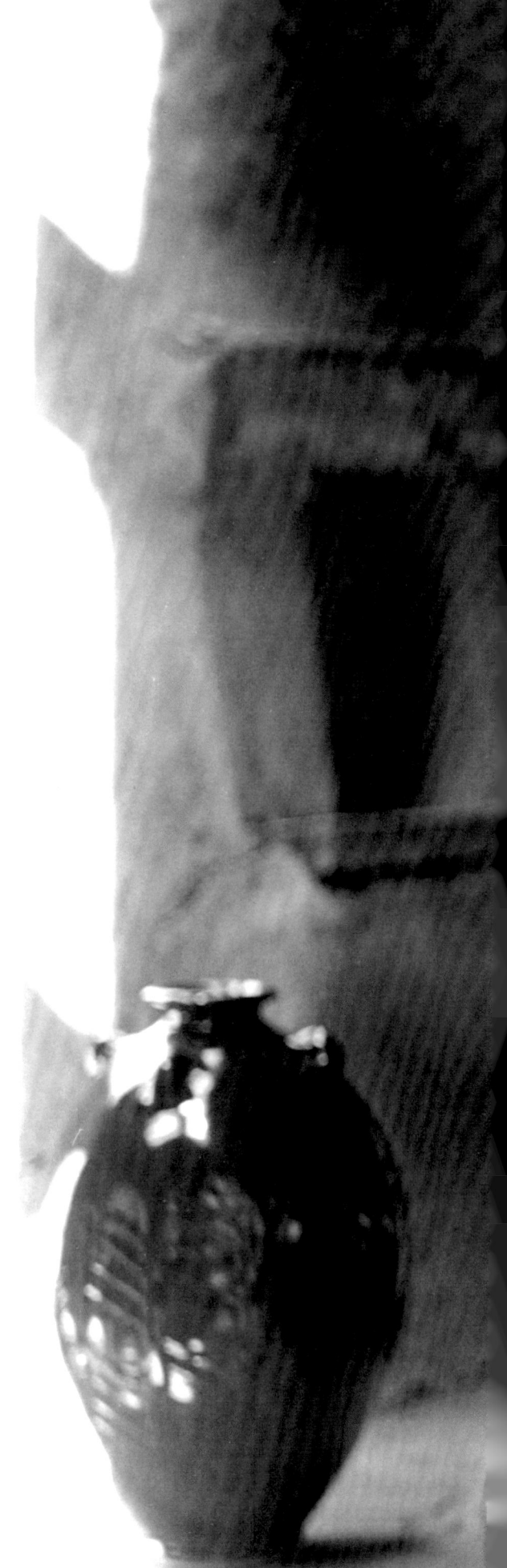

Wayne Ngan
Renowned potter
Hornby Island

a successful, well-known artist, yet on the back of the calendar he was explaining the new directions he hoped to take his art.

One is never too old to develop one's creative talents or imagine new possibilities.

Play hockey into your eighties if you feel like it, even though people may tell you that you should have hung up your skates when you turned fifty. Baseball players can be eighty years old. Ninety-year-olds study at university.

As a surgeon, I have seen many patients in my office who are advanced in chronologic age but ageless in spirit. It is often expected that one retire at around sixty-five. But if you are competent, physically able and still enjoying the work, I encourage you not to retire unless you must and even then not to retire your mind.

Rather, mentor others. Society needs people with the wisdom of experience as well as those with the exuberance of youth.

When your car gets old, its body may be rusty, the tires may be worn down. In other words, it may be time to 're-tire' your vehicle. But this doesn't necessarily mean taking the car off the road and replacing it with another, younger

Between the Links

model. It may mean replacing the tires, repairing the rust and carrying on.

Remain actively communicative. Reveal your unique being to others, so that they might also be enriched by observing you.

All around you are questions. Contemplate them without needing the answers. Discover the magic in framing each moment from where you stand, knowing this moment and your perspective of it will change each time you move.

Be true to your own beliefs and follow your desires, regardless of your age.

What do chains, of themselves, represent?

Chains hold things together, but they can also trap, preventing freedom, expression and creativity. When chains are put into a box they are neutralized, preventing their ability to be useful or restrictive. Out of the box, they can be tightened, loosened or broken, for good or ill intent.

Maybe we can break the chains we create for ourselves and then learn to survive and even thrive between the links. Perhaps it is here that all possibility for free expression exists.

The Muse

Skin Deep

Our view of people is often superficial. How would we react if we could see the whole person — brain, intestines, heart and lungs — and then also be granted greater understanding of the psyche that makes up this person's mind and spirit?

Our awareness of ourselves is often very different from how others see us. We become vulnerable and uncomfortable when we see ourselves on video or hear our own voice. We ask ourselves, who is the real me? And as we age, who is that old person in the mirror?

We mustn't conform to others' ideas of how we should be or look but instead determine our own sense of self. As Oscar Wilde wrote, "Be yourself; everyone else is already taken."

Our Experience of Time

Growing up, I often thought of time as past, present and future. I now know that none of these realms can be truly experienced. The past is gone, the future yet to be. The present is the only feasible place to exist, but it is elusive, for as soon as one tries to grasp it, time has already slipped into the past.

What, then, do we experience when we live 'in the present'?

By 'the present' we really mean an event that includes a portion of the past and the future as well as the current moment. Your spouse calls and asks, "Will you be home soon?" You respond that you are "on your way now." The present is not simply an instant, but also includes

Past, Present, Future

the immediate past (the first part of your movement toward home) and the immediate anticipated future (in arriving there).

Our awareness of the passage of time is directly related to the number of events we experience and the intervals between them. In some instances, time passes quickly — such as when one is under anesthesia, or during deep sleep. To our mind, time stands still during these periods, and it seems we move from past to future almost instantaneously.

If, however, a person is awake when they should be asleep and aware of the ticking clock, time passes very slowly indeed, and the night will seem very long. When everything is still, time can sometimes feel like it is eternal.

"How did it get so late so soon." – Dr. Seuss

On the other hand, when a person is engrossed in a single event, they can become oblivious to everything else around them, including the passing of time. This state of being is almost meditative and can be blissful, resulting in time 'flying by'.

Time is a progression. It can take months or years to evolve a concept or to create something new.

The dilemma of time is difficult to grasp. All states, past, present and future, are valid and powerful realities. Albert Einstein believed that the distinction between them was arbitrary, that there exists only a single continuum of time and space defining the events of the universe.

Many of my photographs contain lines that extend into in sky or water. I have been intrigued by this sense of reality that, while grounded, leads into the unknown. Will these never-ending lines continue into another dimension? Or will these lines be accountable to the confines of this reality and weather with the nature of time, to disappear at a particular point after we have contemplated them?

The Climb

Into the Unknown

Nature of Time

Richmond Skyline, 1973

Richmond Skyline, 1999

Progress?

The Child is Father of the Man

The Child is Father of the Man

Most people believe that adults pass their wisdom on to their children. In his poem "My Heart Leaps Up," however, William Wordsworth reverses this principle, stating that the child is the one who teaches the adult.

My heart leaps up when I behold
A rainbow in the sky:
So was it when my life began;
So is it now I am a man;
So be it when I shall grow old,
Or let me die!
The Child is father of the Man;
And I could wish my days to be
Bound each to each by natural piety.

Our Youngest

Life starts in infancy with enjoyable innocence. As one grows into adulthood it is more difficult to hold onto this purity of seeing, and existence often appears distorted and the world corrupt. Wordsworth vowed to carry the childhood experience of beauty with him his whole life, and I can recall three personal episodes that brought home this lesson for me.

Years ago, my family took a trip to Seattle. I parked our van under a bridge where several derelict men were lying in long trench coats. As we started walking toward the city, Linda noticed that our eight-year-old son, Hershel, had dropped a five-dollar bill from his pocket. When she drew this to his attention, he asked her to keep it quiet. He had dropped the money on purpose, with the hope that the men under the bridge would find it and assume it had been lost by accident. He respected their dignity and wanted no recognition for his action. Without being taught, Hershel was instinctively embodying the Jewish concept of Tikkun Olam, social justice and the repair of the world.

Years later, his own son, Jonah, was drawing an eagle. When Hershel asked him about it, Jonah said the eagle was flying up into the sky, plucking diamonds out of the clouds and taking them down to earth for the people who needed them.

Very recently, our granddaughter Allegra said to my wife: "Grandma, we don't need any presents, we just want your love."

We must look to our children and their clear, open minds in order to see the world without memory and to learn to let go of judgment. Children know. They do not spend their time focused on negativity.

We each have an inner child that sometimes breaks through the box of our adult, learned, societal values. When we allow this breakthrough to happen, we find we are able to express ourselves more freely.

"It's never too late to have a happy childhood."
– Tom Robbins

A Beautiful Family

Grover's Birthday Speech

Written by myself, Linda and our children

Dear friends and human relatives,

Thank you for coming to my 134th birthday. In fact, if you multiply 7 times 18 human years you get 126 dog years, not 134 as stated by the management! I hate it when people make me older than I really am! As I am sure you all know, my real birthday is not until November, but I think it was a good thing to have the party early just in case. (You never know at my age!)

Dogs have asked me on my daily walks how it feels to be so old. And I tell them, I feel great! Not a day over 120! I've been treated so well that when I was young and foolish, I thought I was a god. It wasn't until years later that I realized I was just dyslexic!

I must say that I have had a very exciting life thus far. I loved jumping off that thirty-foot cliff at Lighthouse Park. It was almost like skydiving! And that time I scared the hell out of my human family when I chased the cars on the highway. The most fun was watching the look on their faces when every time they tried to catch me, I ran away farther and chased a few more cars! What fun!

The other time I had them freaked out was when I went merrily hopping along the beach on Hornby and a rather big eagle decided he would like to eat me for lunch! I still dipsy-doodled along the sand and had a great time teasing the bird and scaring my family.

I am very well-liked in our area and have gotten to know many of Shaughnessy's finest derrieres. One of these likes to phone my human family and call the police every time I say a word. (So much for freedom of speech.) I feel right at home, and on my walks, I like to spread my influence all over the neighbourhood.

I would like to make a confession to my human parents: I am really a cross between a miniature poodle and a bunny rabbit! It has been a secret all these years. So now you know.

Against my will, I have led a life of celibacy. This is a shame, considering how attractive I am, except for my chin. (You may call me a diamond in the woof!)

At this point, I think I'll stop. . .for a moment. Someone told me I could make my speech really dramatic if I used my pause (did they mean 'paws'?).

I really have no complaints about my adopted human parents. The food has been okay, especially Friday night dinners (in particular the entire turkey and sixteen baked potatoes), and the cookies pretty tasty. The exercise has been a bit erratic, but I understand that my human dad sometimes has to operate on other humans when he should really be taking me for a walk! Who's more important?

I really only have one main grievance. After all, how would you like to take orders from people fifty years younger than you—even if they are your parents?

I would like to take a moment to remember my sister, Ginger, who passed on last year at the ripe old age of 119. I miss her very much, although I was insanely jealous of her. (I threw a complete hissy fit when my new brother, Chaim, appeared on the scene. Here's a toast to him — "le Chaim, le Chaim!")

As you may know, in my honour the washroom facilities for this party will be where I love to go — namely the dining room rug! Please refrain from going anywhere else, such as the lawn. (Heaven forbid!)

So, all in all, it's been a pretty good life. Sometimes I wish I had a bigger brain, like the humans claim to, so I could maybe understand and appreciate how they see things. However, when I see how much most of them use their brains, I'm not really all that envious.

Besides, doggone it, how many humans can say they lived as long as me?

Play

How Less Can Be More

I once had a medical colleague who was born in India and related to me the story of his childhood and how he came to Canada.

He was raised in a small village. His parents were farmers and, like everyone else in the town, dirt poor and struggling to keep bread on the table. The only toys he had were the stones he collected from the roadside, until his parents gave him a set of paints he could use to colour the stones. He walked to and from school (which was also a temple) where his only teacher was an elderly man who taught him English and math in return for something to eat.

When he was ten, his family moved to Canada, a land that for them represented riches and opportunity. It was a culture shock and he promised himself that one day he would save up enough money to go back home.

In spite of the abject poverty he experienced as a child, with none of the toys considered standard fare for Canadian kids, he fondly remembered those days as being full of joy, contentment and magic.

As time went on and his family became established in Canada, his dream to return to India faded. He eventually went on to study medicine as a young adult and start a family of his own.

Years later, he returned to his hometown in India for a visit and was struck by what he saw. Walking down the street, which was just as sparse and impoverished as he remembered it, he was amazed at the smiles on the faces he passed. This was something he was not used to in Canada, where people, despite having almost anything they wanted materially, seemed often dissatisfied and unhappy.

His story offers a valuable illustration of how material things do not necessarily bring contentment. Indeed, they often have the opposite effect.

From his story I learned that I do not need to have many possessions. If a person has the basic necessities of life and can refrain from seeking what they don't have, life becomes much simpler, with less clutter — both physical and mental — and less stress. This in turn enables a person to spend time on important non-material things like creativity, family and friendship.

More is not always more. Less is not always less.

Look Beyond

What Goes Around Comes Around

Seventy years ago, I was told how to pronounce my grandfather's Yiddish name, Zaida. I tried repeatedly and unsuccessfully, and what came out was "Asia." From then on, that became my grandfather's adopted name for all the grandchildren and the rest of the family.

Fast-forward sixty-five years. My first grandchild, Allegra, tried to pronounce my new name, Grandpa. Just as I a generation before, she couldn't quite manage it. Out came "Pumpa," my new name forevermore, for all my eleven grandchildren. Soon Lev and Zava renamed my favourite snack "pumpcorn," and Aliya came along to call me Pumps. Rafa's magical drawing of a horn-bee came with an "I love you, Pumpy."

What goes around comes around, Asia.

Generation to Generation

Satisfaction

I find far more satisfaction in a goal achieved through the investment of time and effort than in effortlessly acquiring an object with a high price tag. Part of the pleasure of life is derived from accomplishing objectives with one's own actions. A young person who purchases a second-hand car they had to work and save for will appreciate it far more than someone who is simply given the gift of an expensive vehicle.

The anticipation, planning and preparation for a trip are often more pleasurable than the arrival at your destination. To fly to the top of a mountain by helicopter is one thing. To climb there with ropes and crampons is another.

Digital photography has made making images easy — almost effortless — but for me there is nothing like sweating it out in the darkroom, agonizing over the nuances of grey tones that go into a beautiful black and white print. The process of making the print is where the excitement in creating something new is experienced.

I endeavoured to pass the pursuit of this kind of satisfaction on to my children, nurturing them as they learned to crawl, walk and then run. Sometimes they struggled, but as they took their next steps, they reached a sense of accomplishment that continues to affect their confidence and feelings of self-worth.

"If you quit on the process, you are quitting on the result."
– Idowu Koyenikan

The Art of Life

The art of life is not about what appears to be real, true or false, what is convenient or what is self-gratifying. The art of life is about gathering knowledge and then discovering something new or innovating on what has already been uncovered in order to enhance one's experience of reality.

Life cannot be experienced without room for nuance. All things are approximate and representative. Question what you can never be certain of. Even a preconditioned attitude can change through the volition to look more closely at new possibilities. The art of life is also a science, and science needs creativity.

Artists experiment with the mind and the heart. Through trial and error, the artist may innovate with colour, form, technique, light and representation. In the darkroom, the photographer as artist will carefully select the chemical developer to bring new consciousness from the darkness into the light.

To succeed in the art of life, one must move to discover and then experiment with deepening insight.

"The greatest artists are scientists too."
– Albert Einstein

The Chair in Nature

The Chair in Culture

Lessons from Nature

We once put a bird feeder on our porch. Watching the way the birds approached the feeder raised some interesting questions in my mind about the nature of humanity, compared to the operations of the natural world.

There was no conflict when the sparrows landed on the perch and each took their bite or two of the seed mixture. In fact, the whole process appeared quite well organized. There were almost never two birds at the feeder at the same time. One would come and peck, and as that bird left, another would move in, and so on. They each seemed to respectfully wait their turn until the former had finished.

I also noticed that the swallows did not appear randomly. There were either no swallows at all or several waiting in a nearby tree. I had the feeling there was a definite social network among them.

In time, two large black birds with a deep 'croaking' voice came to eat the seeds that had spilt on the ground under the feeder. These ravens always appeared in pairs, something I also thought was no coincidence, and I imagined them to be mates. One would perch in the tree above, protectively keeping watch while the other ate.

Then once, an entire group of crows appeared, calling out with their raucous voices. Watching them, I realized that they all started to caw at once when warding off a perceived threat — our dog, Simba, coming into the yard. Clearly the crows were standing guard while others ate.

Upon research, I learned that crows, with their seemingly simple "caw, caws," have a vocabulary of over 250 sounds. There is a connection between these birds that goes beyond survival.

Studying the birds, I began to think about human psychology and to reflect on what binds living beings together. Can it be extended to protect our entire world community?

Open to the Light

Respecting Animals

Once, our bird feeder was attacked by a squirrel. The feeder was hanging by a rope tied to a branch on a tree near our back porch. I watched the squirrel climb to a higher branch, grab on with its hind legs, dangle the rest of its body upside down and feed away on the seeds in the feeder.

We tried lowering the feeder to make this more difficult. What did the squirrel do?

He examined the new position of the feeder and seemed to realize that it presented a problem. He went to an even higher branch and then to several other locations on the tree to size up the situation. Then, he gave up.

The squirrel, by making some calculations, estimating whether or not he should do a trial run, was behaving like we do when confronted with a big problem. When making complex decisions, the prefrontal cortex in the human brain is stimulated. This allows us to avoid dangerous or unpleasant consequences by preconceiving a situation without actually having to act. For a creature considered to be intellectually 'inferior' to humans, this squirrel was very clever.

We human beings tend to think of ourselves as superior to what we call 'the animals'. Of course, we too are part of the animal kingdom. Although we appear to have certain characteristics in the intellectual realm that give us advantages, many other species are also intelligent and boast other abilities that far exceed those of humans.

A grasshopper is approximately two inches long on average yet can jump thirty inches! If humans could jump as far as grasshoppers do, relative to size, then we could leap more than the length of a football field.

An ant can carry ten to fifty times its body weight. Dogs know a person is arriving at the house long before their owner can hear a thing. Whales communicate with each other underwater over incredible distances.

Fish can survive underwater indefinitely. Birds can fly. Humans cannot do any of these things without the assistance of complex technology.

We need to realize with humility that we are only one part of the larger animal kingdom. Valuing and having respect for all living creatures is essential to our own well-being.

Of course, people vary widely in their talents and abilities. No human is superior in all things. Likewise, in the animal kingdom, all creatures have unique adaptive strengths that have enabled them to survive in their environments. In spite of our different capabilities, we all, humans and non-humans alike, have value.

We all feel, think, communicate and have perception. It is clear, however, that within humankind the individual level of 'awareness' and resulting conscience vary greatly. We have no way of knowing what it feels like to be a whale, an ant, a seagull or any other life form. At each birth, a new consciousness comes into this world having no say as to what creature they will embody. All life forms should be respected and protected from suffering.

Our physical freedom evolves within the confines of time, space and chance, but there is no limit to the freedom of imagination or compassion. By widening our consciousness to embrace other life forms, we may no longer find ourselves quite so alone.

"All his life he tried to be a good person. Many times, however, he failed. For after all, he was only human. He wasn't a dog."
– Charles M. Schulz

Mistakes

The biggest challenge in life is to know yourself, accept yourself and then overcome what you can of your failings. Often people do not self-reflect or become introspective enough to observe their own mental and emotional processes. But if you can't see what needs to be worked upon, it is hard to surmount the obstacles that hinder your happiness.

Nothing in the world is perfect. Making mistakes is inevitable. If one agrees with this premise, then it is much easier to accept the errors we commit, forgive ourselves and apologize when appropriate.

Accepting our failings is a sign of our own progress. Evolving our consciousness, we may learn not to make the same errors, but know this: as long as we are a part of the world, we will make other mistakes. In the process we may gain humility. Allow mistakes to be opportunities for self-reflection and growth.

Rings of Life

Cut Down

Protection

There exists within us an important mechanism for protecting the body from physical destruction: pain.

Without the ability to experience pain, people would continually cause themselves injury. A person avoids putting their hand on a hot stove or into a fire so as to avoid the unpleasantness. The result is avoidance of a severe burn. This helps to preserve not only individuals, but the species as a whole.

There is an equivalent mechanism at work in the human psyche.

If a person breaks the 'rule' to not put one's hand in the fire, the result is physical pain. If a person breaks a moral 'rule', the result is an emotional injury. Guilt is a mechanism, taught from a young age, that aids people in acting morally. The painful feeling helps us to do better the next time an opportunity arises. But guilt can also be a response to one's inability to do so.

Addressing moral shortcomings in one's own nature may result in more kindness toward oneself and others and thereby aid in soothing our all-too-human attributes.

Appreciation

A friend recently sent me a link to a YouTube video that I found enchanting.

It was a scene in which a street musician — a bass player — started to play his instrument with the apparent aim of attracting a crowd and presumably some cash. Indeed, the people in the street began to gather around him. He was playing a familiar tune, the last movement of Beethoven's Ninth Symphony.

Before long, a cellist walked up and joined the bass player. As the piece progressed, more and more performers appeared and began to play their respective parts, until there was a whole orchestra, complete with conductor and chorus, playing in all its glory. The crowd was captivated, the video showing images of smiling children laughing and hanging from lampposts.

I was so enthralled by the whole event that I sent it around to my friends and family, expecting them to react as I did. I was not prepared for their response.

It was pointed out that this was not the charming, spontaneous and joyful event I had thought it to be. They brought to my attention the fact that the video took place in front of an Italian Bank, the name of which was boldly visible to those who cared to notice. The sudden appearance of an entire symphony orchestra on the street was clearly rehearsed and planned, something that should have been obvious to anyone watching.

I had not even thought about how unlikely it was that a set of cameramen was miraculously present to record the whole event.

Not everything is as it appears. However, I still think it is good to be grateful for gifts received, no matter where they came from or how they were produced, as long as they are uplifting and cause no harm.

Seeking Repair

Bad things in life are not to be avoided. All human beings experience hardship and pain. By accepting this and welcoming life's challenges as opportunities from which to learn and grow and heal, then "The wound [becomes] the place where the light enters you," as the poet Rumi says.

If possible, it is best to face painful experiences as they occur. Be with your pain. Then, when able to move ahead, it is helpful not to fixate on those experiences or hold on to them too tightly. Lingering feelings of hurt will likely lessen with time.

Once able, step into the light again, for the possibility of repair exists here.

You may find the idea of Tikkun Olam to be relevant in these times. According to these teachings, self-growth is gained from repeated acts of helping others, especially those who might be hurting even more than oneself.

The Storm

Pond Dance

Reflecting Light in the Forest
(previous image)

Ripple Effect

When one throws a pebble into a lake, an initially small ripple grows and spreads out over the water. It might intersect with ripples from stones thrown by others.

Similarly, one encouraging or negative remark can have a ripple effect upon a person, ultimately influencing how they see themselves amidst a sea of others.

Honour your own ripple and make your own distinctive waves. Try to have your ripple maintain its innate integrity when intersecting with others, while at the same time realizing that you are part of something bigger, a vital and driving force of energy, going where you wish to go while affecting all the other elements in your midst.

Even as your ripple stills, you are always part of the constant flow of the universe.

Meeting Shore

A Double-Edged Sword

Arguably a most important and useful invention by man, the knife can kill and skin animals, can be used to harvest and prepare food and cut cardboard and bindings. A knife can wound or cut, but a knife in the form of a scalpel can save lives. Such similar instruments, used in different ways — a double-edged sword.

Sometimes, walking through life can be likened to walking on a tightrope. One must maintain a semblance of calm while balancing between opposing elements: light and darkness, love and hate, right and wrong. Excess one way or another can prove detrimental. When performing surgery, one must wield the scalpel with the utmost care in order to not make one small slip.

It is a balancing act. As a surgeon and a human being, I know too well — it is all a matter of the care and purpose for which we use the knife.

Being Humble

In our competitive world, humility is not always viewed as a positive attribute. When a society values sensationalism and excess, humility is not a trait that is encouraged.

On the other hand, when a person is described as outstanding in a particular field and then it is noted that they are humble or modest in their demeanour, they are more highly regarded.

The truth is, no matter how hard you try to be the best in anything you do, there is always something still to learn.

Each person should strive to place themselves into the context of the world. Each of us is one of billions on this planet. No matter whether we are prideful or humble, or a combination of both, the natural process of time will eventually level us all.

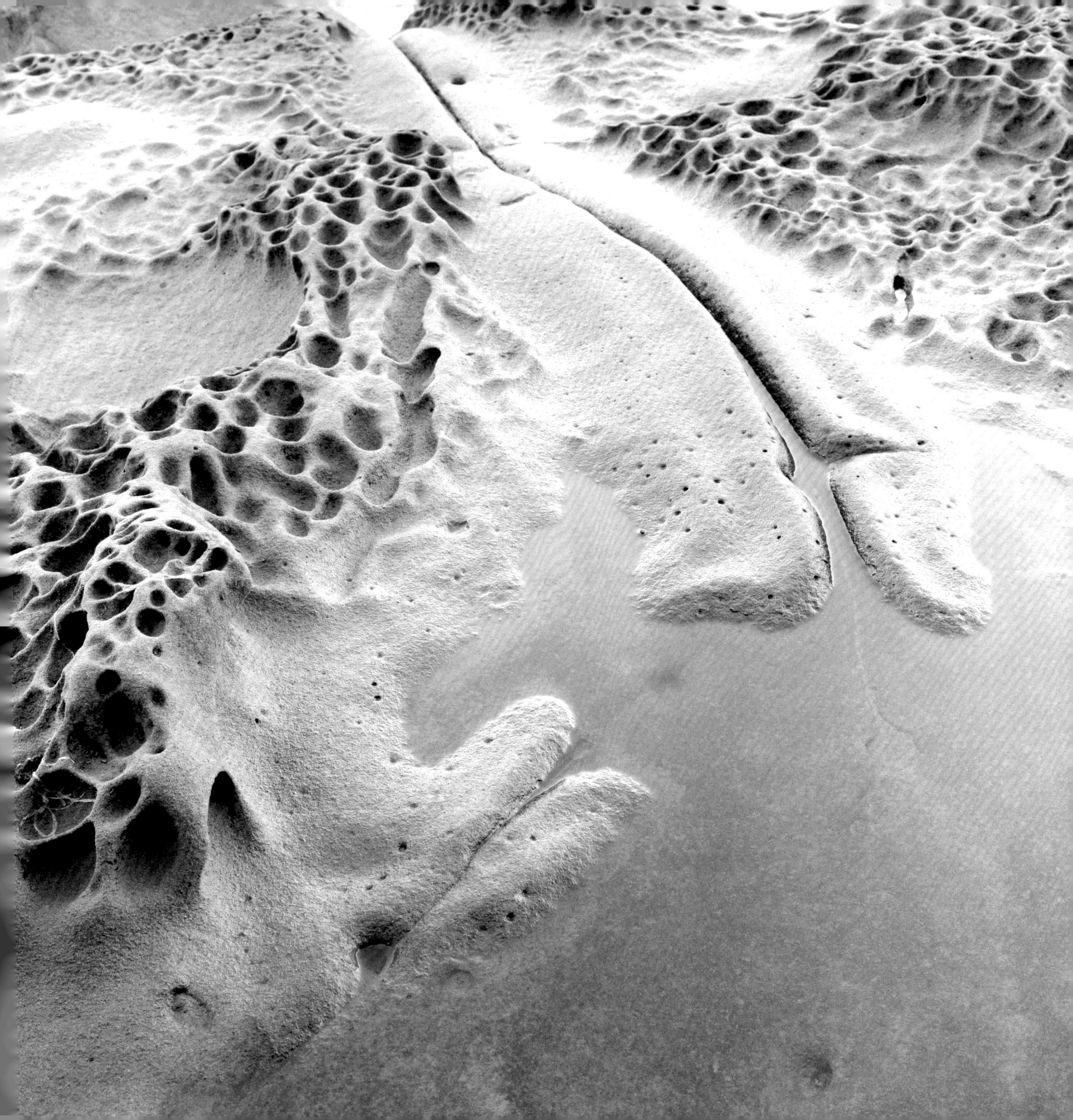

Sandcastles

Many children make sandcastles on the beach at low tide, often competing for the biggest, highest and most beautiful by decorating them with shells, driftwood and weathered broken glass.

In the heat of competition, some may try to knock over or destroy those of their competitors.

Despite their attachment to these fairy-tale structures, the tide inevitably comes in and washes all of them away.

As with the tides, life is cyclical. Nothing is permanent. All of our castles will one day disappear, and as it is with sand on the beach, we will all end up on an even shore.

Shore

Challenge Yourself

There are countless ways to perceive this earth. Delving into the teeming organic life below the waves when scuba diving opens an enormous other realm. Peering at a sample under a microscope unveils a unique and fascinating miniscule world. Both guide us to a deeper understanding of what lies beneath the surface.

As we walk through life, we have attitudes that hopefully evolve with us. We may choose to shelter ourselves, we may contemplate adventure into the unknown or we may remain contentedly in place. Exploring our natural curiosity enables our minds to acquire understanding and eventually wisdom. Then, through our own creative seeing, we might guide those around us to see more.

Expectation

Many years ago, upon entering a year of medical internship after med school, I was asked to state my top three preferences for placement. I decided that I wanted to stay in a large Canadian city, so my list consisted of Toronto, where I had lived my life thus far with friends and family; Montreal, where my first wife, Vicki, and I had good friends; and Vancouver, a large, unknown city I had never visited, which lay thousands of kilometres away from home.

Toronto and Montreal didn't work out, and so I accepted Vancouver. At the time it seemed a huge disappointment.

In retrospect, it turned out to be one of the greatest things that ever happened to me. We came to love the city and the new friends we made. I discovered then how 'bad events' in one's life can be turned around and made into something beautiful and positive.

Expectation and disappointment go hand in hand, for the higher one's expectations, the greater the frustration when they are not met.

Try to be realistic with respect to your goals. Shooting for the stars is not a bad thing, for it provides you the hope of one day reaching them. However, it is prudent to not "put all of one's eggs in one basket," as the saying goes, and to always have an alternative plan.

It helps to not take life too seriously. Think about the actual consequences of not reaching a goal, to help place it in a broader perspective. It's usually not the tragedy you initially thought it would be. It might even be possible, with a good attitude, to turn the apparent 'failure' into a positive experience.

Life largely depends on you and what you make of it. Life can be so much more enjoyable when one focuses on what makes it worthwhile.

"Make the most of yourself — for that is all there is of you."
– Ralph Waldo Emerson

As another saying goes, "wherever you go, there you are." Try to be the best you can and not give in to feelings of failure. Become the tree that bends in response to life's forces while always reaching for the sky.

The greatest peace of mind comes when one learns to let go of expectations. *Just let them go.*

Stuck

This photograph was taken in an ancient part of Jerusalem. Symbolically, the man in black is moving through life. He navigates under archways and up and down multiple staircases that, like rites of passage, need to be overcome. Light, symbolic of man's struggle for purpose, beams through an archway above while he is momentarily immobilized, stuck in his own perceptions. If he continues downward, his options become restricted.

He is suspended between dimensions, only able to view what is below him. But if he turns a bit and adjusts his perception, all options become possible.

Stuck

The Path to Wisdom

Having knowledge of something implies the ability to enter facts and experiences into one's conscious mind, where they are retained as memory.

Understanding goes a step further, suggesting insight into what those facts mean and their implications in a broader sense.

Wisdom is the ability to apply this understanding in the world and integrate it into one's life, to the point that it reaches out to teach and touch another being. This is life's pathway.

Transcending

White Light

When light is scattered and broken apart into its separate components, the result is many different colours that are not always complementary, and as such, not always in harmony.

However, when all the different wavelengths of light are combined, the result is pure white light.

The same can be said for our society. With the gradual elimination of boundaries between people and nations, the mingling of different backgrounds can result in a much more illuminated world. Being receptive to differences offers us the opportunity to be empathetic, contributing instruments of creativity.

Similarly, every human being is composed of a complex mix of different psychological traits. At times, aspects of one's nature may be excessive enough to become a source of conflict. A person may obtain greater strength of character when their opposing qualities are brought into balance. With a more unified personality, the person might then — as with the combination of colours that compose white light — bring a clearer and brighter vision to their world.

White Light

Boundless Meadow
(previous image)

Text to Saudi Patient

The myths that we learn to believe when young can have a very negative influence if thought to be absolute truths, especially if they disparage the myths or beliefs of others. This can lead to intolerance and, at worst, tragic hatred and violence. There are abundant examples of such behaviour in our contemporary global landscape. All people have a right to hold their beliefs and have them acknowledged with tolerance, as long as they will not cause harm to others.

In January of 2018, the bodyguard of a Saudi government minister appeared in my Richmond office requesting that I consider fixing his boss's inguinal hernia. The minister had flown to Richmond in his private jet when his daughter was to give birth, and he thought it would be an opportune moment to have the troublesome hernia fixed. Arrangements were made, I performed the surgery and the minister and I subsequently became good friends. We exchanged many texts, including this one from me to him:

With the news lately about Saudi-Canadian relations, I couldn't help but think about my Saudi friend and patient. I hope you are fully recovered from your surgery and back full-time into life! Please let me know how you are doing. I meant to tell you earlier about what it meant to get to know you, even for a short time.

Here we had a Jewish surgeon operating on an Arab official with ease and a wonderful feeling of goodwill and understanding. It brought home what should be an obvious fact: we all come to this earth as innocent babies, we live a few years trying to be happy and perhaps contribute something to make the world a better place, and then we leave and return to the earth as dust.

This does not apply only to people of a particular race, skin colour, belief, financial status or political position. It applies to everyone.

This should teach us humility and respect for all people. It should make us realize that in spite of our superficial differences, on a more profound level, we are all brothers and sisters. What a different world it would be if we interacted with each other as family!

Friend, I want to say that I sensed in you that very thing. It warmed my heart and I thank you for it. I hope that our respective governments can enter into a mature and wise dialogue to resolve the issues at hand, for the good of us all.

Once again, please let me know how you are doing. You should be back into your full exercise routine by now. All the best to you and your family.

Your friend,
Mike

Freedom

Freedom is not easy to define. For those physically confined, it may mean freedom of movement, the ability to go where you want, when you want. For those in servitude, it may mean owning the rights to and profits of their physical labour. For all, equally, our thoughts are free. No one can control what our minds contain unless we let them.

Living in a 'free society' is even harder to define. In society, there is an inherent responsibility to assure that one's personal freedom will not cause harm to others. Negative actions may result in punishment according to the rules of society.

This issue becomes challenging when considering freedom of speech. Should there be a limit on what one says when it is hurtful and prejudiced?

In my view, the rules of society, designed to protect people from harming one another, should apply to all human behaviour, even speech. Often, words can injure a person even more than physical violence.

Whether it is physical or verbal, the line on human behaviour should be drawn not only when life is threatened, but also when there is a real threat of negating others.

On the Dock

Communication

It is generally assumed that the main source of communication between people is language. An English-speaking person will be able to exchange ideas with someone who speaks and understands English, whereas they may find it almost impossible to achieve the same level of understanding with someone who speaks only Mandarin.

Thankfully, we can also communicate non-verbally. A genuine smile and other facial expressions, as well as gestures or body language, can be very effective. In particular, our eyes often communicate a stronger message than anything else. Indeed, even without a shared language, significant communication takes place between animals and humans.

Occasionally it is wise to be economical with our words. Sometimes it is what is not said that has the most value.

Relating

Have a Nice Day

Walking down the hall in the hospital one day, I passed one of the nurses I worked with. We greeted each other with the standard "How are you doing?" and "Have a nice day." I wondered, what do these typical greetings really mean?

I recently parked my car at a meter and paid using "pay by phone." I received a response by text thanking me for the payment and hoping that I would have "a good rest of my day." How sincere and heartfelt was that wish, coming from an automated message?

Every New Year's Eve, I watch a hockey game on television in which the announcer wishes everyone a very healthy and happy new year. He is talking to a camera. Just how personal can his message be?

Let us say that you knew another person had just been diagnosed with metastatic cancer and was to undergo major surgery and chemotherapy. Asking that person how they were doing would carry a lot more weight than if the person was not known to be ill.

When you say, "have a nice day," choose to think about your words and their intention so they are not just superficial platitudes without genuine intent. Do you really hope in your heart that that person is going to have a nice day?

Albert Einstein said, "There are only two ways to live your life. One is as though nothing is a miracle. The other is as though everything is a miracle." If we constantly live without thoughtful intention in our words and actions, there is a danger we will miss out on life's miracles.

Sherlock Holmes

"Let the young know they will never find a more interesting, more instructive book than the patient himself."
– *Giorgio Baglivi*

I'd advise all medical doctors to read and learn from Arthur Conan Doyle's classic stories of Sherlock Holmes. Nothing escapes the attention of the master sleuth, who refers to himself as a consulting detective. He fits his keen, logical observations together to deduce the most amazing things about a person and their life — and this is precisely what a physician should do.

The character of Holmes was inspired by a real-life surgeon named Joseph Bell, who practiced at the Royal Infirmary of Edinburgh and whom Doyle met in 1877 when he worked for him as a clerk. Like the character Holmes, Bell was able to draw specific conclusions from detailed observations.

Doyle writes about the need not only to see, but to really observe. After all, as Holmes says, there is nothing more deceptive than an obvious fact.

Blood work and CT scan images are used to confirm deductions derived by initial clinical observation. To arrive at these conclusions, a doctor must examine the whole person. Talking to them, learning who they really are, helps a physician complete their diagnosis and determine their care.

Opposites Attract

In his book *Of Love and Lust* (1941), Theodor Reik proposed an explanation for the workings of love between two individuals. Everyone, consciously or not, feels a little lost and inadequate. We all wish to be as complete as possible. Love, he wrote, is an attempt to turn this dream into reality.

When two people meet who each appear to have those characteristics the other lacks, their union brings together their individual strengths to create two more complete people.

Likewise, Kabbalah teaches that two souls become one under the wedding canopy when they are united in matrimony. The symbolism of the ring joins them together in a circle without end.

Once within this circle, however, the spiritual relationship with one another will still need work and care. You must continuously follow that circle of love, for it is everlasting.

"*True love stories never have endings.*"
– Richard Bach

Attraction

Tranquil Passage
(previous image)

The Ring

In general, we are more likely to cry when we are sad than when we are happy, yet it is common for people to cry at weddings. Witnesses of this joyous event often shed tears of happiness for the new couple, so much in love and with so much to look forward to. This joy may also bring to light questions about life and the longing for a dream to come true.

In the foreground of this photograph, one can see a hand adorned with a new wedding ring. This part of the picture is in perfect focus, while the softened background represents the subtle complexities that can make a new relationship all the more rewarding.

Imagine

Imagine being alive 120 years ago, when long-distance communication was in its infancy, the rotary telephone barely a dream and smart phones unheard of. What would you have thought then if someone told you that one day a device as small as a deck of cards would enable you to not only talk to another person across the world, but actually see this person speaking to you in real time?

The past 120 years have brought inconceivable advancements. What more does the future hold?

The book whose pages we can touch and feel is easily displaced by a fleeting image behind hard glass. We watch our beautiful HDTVs with their sharpness and rich colours and can forget to listen well to absorb a program's content. Audiophiles sometimes are more concerned with detecting minor nuances of sound, light or colour provided by their latest equipment than with listening to the music itself.

I would rather invest in the vast knowledge that technology offers, without concern for the latest upgraded device.

I would prefer the gift of a meaningful photograph in a simple cardboard box to something without meaning wrapped in an elegant container.

The Dandelions Continue to Grow

Old and New

Remnants Beyond

The Gate

Barkerville Scarecrow

Bring the Past Forward

In history, there are countless examples of how past events continue to fuel conflict among cultures and belief systems today. The past is often misrepresented and used to promote discord amongst people.

At the same time, the beauty and accomplishments of what humankind has achieved, once preserved in our collective memory, enrich us and our communities. Unpredictable and seemingly insurmountable events often offer opportunities for us to cope and gain resilience — to learn from our ancestors' stories.

Bring the Past Forward

Dimensions of Silence

We are seemingly afraid of silence.

When we go for a walk or jog or commute to work, we need to put on our iPods or radios. When we arrive home from a day's work, we switch on the TV to provide background noise. When we meet with people, we fill silence with idle chatter, often of minimal, if any, significance.

In contrast, walking in the woods with nothing intruding on the auditory senses but the sounds of nature can be a calming, perhaps even spiritual, experience.

Calm

When overwhelmed by the noise of the world, return to the silence in nature. This is the place where stress dissolves into awe.

"Nature is pleased with simplicity. And nature is no dummy."
— *Isaac Newton*

Silence has dimensions of its own.

Gordon at his Farm
Hornby Island

The Value of Leisure

Years ago, before the industrial revolution, our society was largely agricultural. Farmers started work in the fields early and finished late in the day. Child labour was common. Free time was not a problem — there was none.

With the widespread use of machines, production became less labour-intensive and people started to have more time on their hands. This has increased to the point where filling 'the void' of our free time has turned into a major industry. 'Leisure time' has turned into a challenge to find ways to erase our spare moments rather than fill them with meaning.

Filling one's leisure time with only passive entertainment is a lost opportunity to be creative.

Einstein's day job was working in a passport office. In his spare time, he dabbled in 'armchair' physical theory. His discovery of the theory of relativity resulted from what one would deem his 'hobby'.

The term 'hobby' implies an activity of lesser importance, a diversion from your 'real work', the work you do to make a living. Nothing could be further from the truth. Throughout my lifetime, I've engaged in many pursuits and interests. One might call them 'hobbies', but for me, they are experiences that have creatively inspired my life.

I have gardened, sung in choirs, enjoyed a collection of classical music, pursued woodworking, been a Hornby woodsman and builder, played guitar, collected fanny packs from our travels around the world, read avidly and invented a medical device.

My love of photography and having my own darkroom has allowed me to be a creator,

Boats at Bay

watching the magic of film negatives bring remarkable images to life. Each image is a story, and these stories always amaze me. Whether the process is frustrating or elating, the result is always astonishing.

If you are involved in photography for a living, there is an expectation that you will perform as an expert in this field, whether or not the project is important to you personally — for example, being hired to take pictures at a stranger's wedding. When you are being paid by someone to do what is needed for them, your own creative freedom may become restricted.

When you involve yourself in photography as a 'hobby' — which at particularly meaningful times is experienced more like a calling — then whether documenting a culture's oppression, bringing attention to the logging of old-growth forests or taking portraits of people you choose, your art comes from your own savouring of and integrity toward a moment that you have chosen. This frees you to create evocative images that do not have boundaries imposed on them by others.

Perhaps Einstein was only able to make his earth-shattering discoveries because it was his hobby, not confined to the structure of a traditional 'day job'. Perhaps hobbies are best understood as high value activities that affirm one's existence and that make a difference, even if only in one's own life.

Helliwell Arbutus, Hornby

Regeneration

Life ends.

We consider death a negative and sorrowful event, even when referring to a very elderly or terminally ill person. Indeed, many passings are tragic, particularly when a person dies young. Yet what gives the strongest purpose to human life might be its finite nature. Knowing this provides the impetus to get the most out of life while we can.

We too often fight against what is both natural and necessary. People with terminal cancer and in terrible pain need death for relief of their agony. How cruel it would be if that were not a possibility!

Life depends on death for renewal. What would it be like if no one ever died? The cycle of life and death is an amazing system of regeneration, bringing new energy and ideas to the world on an ongoing basis.

Like many other cultures, the First Nations of what is now called North America understand and respect these laws of nature. The totem poles of First Nations of the Pacific Northwest are carved of wood and exposed to the elements with the understanding that they will eventually wither and return to the forest. From nature born, they return back to nature in death.

Virgin land depends on no human. Through cycles of birth, growth, death, decay and regeneration, nature offers us pathways to negotiate and emulate for our time on earth.

Turning Out the Light

At age sixty-seven, I underwent open-heart surgery. When asked how I would feel if I never woke up, I thought about it a moment then responded, "Is the cup of my life more empty or full? Should I look back at all the years of purposeful living, with the beauty of my surgical work, my family, our dogs, friends and the world outside, and be satisfied? Or should I feel remorse about the years that I may not have ahead?"

Turning Out the Light

At age sixty-seven, I underwent open-heart surgery. When asked how I would feel if I never woke up, I thought about it a moment then responded, "Is the cup of my life more empty or full? Should I look back at all the years of purposeful living, with the beauty of my surgical work, my family, our dogs, friends and the world outside, and be satisfied? Or should I feel remorse about the years that I may not have ahead?"

Various religions teach that when a person passes away, the soul leaves the body and disappears into some eternal realm. Their rationale is that the soul cannot disappear into nothingness and must be a part of something everlasting and indestructible. They say that instead of vanishing, the soul becomes part of the universe, existing forever without death or age.

Consider for a moment the electric light bulb.

When the lamp is turned on, light and warmth emanate from the bulb. So long as the electricity is running, energy, in the form of light and heat, continues to radiate. As soon as the lamp is shut off and the current of electricity ceases, the heat and light are gone. Where did they go?

In fact, they went nowhere. The light simply no longer exists. It was dependent on an electrical current and the light bulb filament for life. When the electricity stopped, the light went out.

Perhaps it is so with the human body and 'soul'. It may also be that the existence of the soul depends upon the viability of the physical body. When the blood no longer circulates, when there are no longer any viable brain cells, then maybe the light bulb is extinguished and disappears into nothingness.

The question might then be this: What is the nothingness at the end of our physical existence? And what, then, does 'everything' in this existence constitute? Are they not a part of each other?

"Death is not the opposite of life, but a part of it."
– Haruki Murakami

Celebration of Life

One has to ask, then, what is there to fear at the end of life? The moment of dying is only a minute instant in time. What comes after is oblivion, the equivalent of a deep general anesthetic. In no way should this be considered a time of suffering, but a time of rest.

What comes before the moment of death is what is important. The way people die varies enormously. The death can be a slow, agonizing one such as might be experienced with metastatic cancer, or it might be very sudden, resulting from an acute myocardial infarction or car accident. Fortunately, with the advanced medical science of today, palliation of possible suffering is a reality and, in most instances, can alleviate almost all pain.

The most important parts of a person's life are the years they spent taking part in the human condition. I see this as twofold: the first is what a person can take from life in the way of positive experience, and the second is what one can give back to humanity and the world to make it a better place.

Not all of life is positive, but the key is to try to have the positives surpass the negatives, so that one can say before death that the overall experience was that of a 'happy life'.

Happiness comes from appreciating what one has and not being envious over what others might have. It leads to an appreciation of life's beautiful and often cherished intricacies, the ones that seem to belong only to you.

"Knowing you have everything is to be truly happy."
– *the Tao Te Ching*

Every person has the capacity to help make the world a better place. If one is successful in contributing with empathy, kindness, creativity and wisdom in even a small way, then this would be a significant factor in making one's life a success.

Doing my small part in the repair of the world — by gluing a broken vase back together, repairing a broken floor or performing a life-saving surgical procedure has given me a sense

Layering

At One

of service. This is one of the reasons I loved my work as a surgeon — the positive outcome for a patient was clear and occurred with almost every operation.

I believe that in most instances, death should not be a cause for grief but rather celebration of the positive aspects of the life that is no longer. The only justifiable sadness is that of the permanent loss of close connection the person had with relatives and friends.

What a person should be aiming for in their final years is to come to peace with the worth in the life they led and to live their final days with acceptance and a great appreciation for the opportunity to have lived it.

As hard as it may seem at the time, this life well-lived should be celebrated at a funeral and not mourned. The light might have gone out, but the glow from each radiant being will live on in those who loved them.

The Meaning of Life

What is the meaning of life?

The answer to this question is elusive. Perhaps one day the box I envisioned will finally be opened and the ultimate truth will be revealed. For now, however, there may be ways of moving closer to finding answers by defining some characteristics of what 'meaning' might look like.

Here are a few ideas:

The 'meaning of life' should be considered in terms of consciousness. All life forms have a certain level of consciousness, but 'meaning' cannot exist without a human being creating and then experiencing it. It is my belief that once a person dies, human consciousness ceases. This consciousness includes not only cognitive functioning, but also emotions and thus, matters of the heart.

An analogy: Consider the value of a blank piece of paper, three by six inches in size. One could postulate that the value of such an item is almost zero. Let us then add to the equation some ink and a pen, both also of very little value. Add words of endearment on this paper and its value increases substantially.

Let us say that the blank piece of paper is inscribed by the Government of Canada as a $1,000 bill. That blank piece of paper now has a large value, so long as a human being can benefit from it.

In and of itself, money is simply a piece of paper, a disc of metal or a number on an account or in a ledger. These objects and representations alone have little or no value. Their worth exists in their potential to impact a person's life, particularly his or her psyche.

The 'value in life' requires two things: a human being, instilling meaning, and another person, experiencing the value of that meaning. It makes sense, then, to attempt to define the value of living (or 'the meaning of life') by examining the self in relation to another. Perhaps living a

Looking Back at History

life enriched by meaning through another person is what makes existence worthwhile.

A significant problem, however, arises when life's experiences bring pain rather than happiness and well-being. Occasionally, difficulties may appear insurmountable. Yet overcoming these difficulties contains the possibility to transform a negative experience into something more positive. However, this is not always the case when it comes to one's health.

If one is elderly and painful health challenges become irreversible, then the question "Is life worth living?" becomes extremely timely. If all that is left in a person's life is physical suffering, why prolong this misery? The end is inevitable and out of our control. The process of getting there is not. We offer euthanasia to animals when circumstances become despairing, out of love and compassion for them. Recently, physician-assisted suicide began to find a place in our human dilemma.

Some schools of thought propose an outside, imposed source of meaning to life, that there is in fact a force, called 'God', which decided to create matter out of nothingness.

If this were the case, then it is conceivable the development of organic matter and living things, including human beings, was all part of an ultimate purpose that 'God only knows'. In human terms, 'living' could then be seen as having an ultimate purpose. This, of course, is one of the reasons we have created religions — to try to explain, among other things, the phenomenon of being alive.

A very significant problem arises with this theory. If we postulate that the universe came into being at the creation of an entity ('God'), then one must eventually ask the question, who created God? And this question would have to be asked ad infinitum.

Perhaps one day we will find the answers we seek. In the meantime, not knowing what is in the box, perhaps it would be best if we accepted that life is a mystery. One thing we know: while in this world, value is to be gained by helping others.

People seem to need a purpose and structure in their lives in order to carry on from day to day, to 'give their lives meaning'. One trains in a profession in order to support their family, while another purchases tools such as a hammer and screwdriver to construct things. Some stay home to raise children and work to make the home more comfortable.

But everything eventually changes. One retires, the thing constructed breaks and home is downsized.

It is how one creates purpose that matters. Purpose entails having the courage to follow your dreams and believe in them enough to let them lead you to more purpose, even when it changes form. Purpose is a process.

"He who has a why to live can bear almost any how."
– Friedrich Nietzche

The ultimate purpose of life remains elusive and possibly without an answer. Meanwhile, we develop a series of goals, realizing that everything that enters our life provides us with an opportunity to evolve purpose and achieve these goals. You can't always see results right away, but while you are trying to achieve them, goals help to create more meaning.

"The meaning of life is whatever you ascribe it to be. Being alive is the meaning."
– Joseph Campbell

At Peace

The words of the great Mexican poet Amado Nervo have been both comforting and inspiring at this time in my life.

At Peace

Very close to my sundown,
I bless your life,
because you never gave me false hope,
nor unjust work,
nor undeserved punishment;
because I see
at the end of my rough path
that I was the architect
of my own destiny;
if I extracted the sweetness
or bitterness of things,
it was because I put bitterness and sweetness
into them:
when I planted rose bushes,
I always reaped roses.
Surely, winter
will follow my vim and vigour —
but you never told me that May would last forever!
I found without a doubt
the nights long with my sorrows,
but you didn't promise me
just good nights,
and instead
I had some of them blessed and serene.
I loved, I was loved,
the sun caressed my face.
Life, you owe me nothing!
Life, we are at peace.

Garden Steps

Look Beyond

I was talking to my daughter a few months ago about my valve replacement that had occurred years earlier and how my health had declined over the following decade. I had also suffered a critical pneumonia in one of my hospitalizations, during which I needed to be on 100 percent oxygen and in intensive care. As my muscles weakened and cognition changed — partly due to the serious drugs I was taking — I suffered multiple falls, breaking both my clavicle and my hip.

At the onset of my illness, I suffered a grave depression, not only because I felt fearful and poorly almost all the time, but also because I had to close my surgical practice and abruptly stop performing surgery and seeing patients.

Up to this point, my life had been filled with purpose and service. The change was a difficult new reality to accept.

I lost my ability to be a surgeon and then, because of temporal lobe epilepsy, my ability to drive. Yet I was surprised that my sudden loss of autonomy also brought me flashes of greater insight.

I realized I needed to live by my basic good principles and values every pain-free day. I needed to look beyond my loss at what I still had, and when I did, I saw action.

I saw my wife, Linda, whose words of affection were being put into action by her constant loyal and devoted care of me.

I saw my children and grandchildren, hovering affectionately near during my bad days and offering me love and caring, and I understood that they were future caregivers.

I saw the love and support that my beloved sister and her husband and my brother and his wife put into action through their phone calls and concern for me every day.

I experienced the caring in ongoing visits from our group of remarkable friends.

Action.

I don't want to spend any more of these next years regretting the things I did not manage to accomplish.

I have received enormous pleasure from the discovery of a new piece of music or from listening over and over again to a piece that I know by heart, that still moves me to tears. I still listen with the intention to respond, for there is so much yet to be discovered by listening well.

From all that I have lost, I am privileged to experience the action of being loved. As I listen to classical music, take short walks, look through our photographs and take more images, I try to absorb each moment of life, understanding that some meaningful things are fleeting, not all can be caught through the lens of a camera or absorbed through sounds that spill into the soul.

Looking beyond my present confinement, I am brought to tears at the astonishing fact of an airplane being able to fly and a mother duck teaching her thirteen babies to swim in our backyard pool.

The world is vast and chaotic, and yet each particle within it slips into place for a time. I may never know what is in the box, but my curiosity will keep me trying to find out every day of my life.

So, I tell you: look beyond.

Look beyond your immediate environment, which is so limited, and try to be aware of the vastness of the world, the universe and the endless unknown.

Look beyond what people say, to the intention in their words.

Look beyond how a person appears, to how he or she finds purpose as a contributing member of society.

Look beyond the pain of past experiences, to what may be learned from them in the future.

Look beyond preconceptions and the inclination to fit everything into a neat box.

Look at the world as if you were seeing it for the first time. Try to do this every day, and you will avail yourself of the possibility to experience more.

Afterword

My husband, Michael, is a modern-day Renaissance man— an explorer who seeks the treasures of the mind and never tires in his pursuit of wisdom. Unafraid to look past boundaries that others perceive as impenetrable, Michael sees beyond objective referents and society as it is typified in the real world. His unique ideas are an opening for us to look more intensely at the mystery of this existence and then focus on the innumerable possibilities within it.

For Michael, the greatest gift has been having the ability to use his mind, heart and hands in service to others. His passion for surgery afforded him the opportunity to alleviate suffering and to save lives.

During his long surgical career spanning more than fifty years, with most spent at his beloved Richmond General Hospital, Michael never gave up on a patient. He looked at each from multiple perspectives to investigate often confounding and intimately unique issues — much like his favourite sleuth, Sherlock Holmes, would have done. Thinking beyond the box, while preserving a patient's dignity, Michael confronted illness, calmed fears and addressed concerns with great integrity, strength and compassion. Taking a humanistic approach to medicine, he recognized the value and agency of each human being.

Seeing life in multiple dimensions, Michael became a multi-dimensional human being himself. His many interests are more like 'callings' than hobbies, as he approaches them with genuine commitment. He is a classical music lover with a vast knowledge and collection of works. He sang in excellent choirs, including the University of Toronto choir and the Vancouver Cantata Singers. He is an avid reader, an inventor of a medical device, a musician, a gardener, a Hornby woodsman and builder and a remarkable photographer, developing beautiful black and white images in his own darkroom.

Michael's search to understand more of this existence is pragmatically viewed through the lens of his camera. While he approaches each subject with intense focus, he sees the tender nuances and captures them in a delicate and rich luminosity. His images are extraordinary moments containing dimensions of seeing that elevate reality to include a sense of the spiritual. Through this depth of seeing, Michael succeeds in transcending himself.

The contrasting emotional tones and thoughtful observations Michael expressed through black, white and grey images and words in this book, have been profoundly influenced by the advice of the great portrait photographer Yousuf Karsh, who remarked, "Look and think before opening the shutter. The heart and mind are the true lens of the camera."

Michael has faced many health challenges within the last two years, but during this time the desire to share his photographic art and pursuit of meaning has been of paramount importance and a source of great purpose. Recently I came upon a short story he had written about Bubby, his grandmother. She, for everyone in our large, blended family of eight children, was an extraordinary compilation of strength, sweetness, wisdom and love. His letter to her also speaks of Michael's nature.

Together in the Woods
—*Michael Frimer, with tripod*

Five years ago, Bubby visited us in Vancouver. After a family brunch in her honour, when cleaning up the dishes, my wife, Linda, went to sweep into the garbage a whole hardboiled egg from someone's plate that was covered in strawberry sauce. Not being one to waste food, I picked the egg out of the garbage, washed it, and was about to put it back in the fridge when Linda expressed disagreement with what I was doing. Bubby, then ninety-one years old, quietly walked over and asked me to show her the egg. Then, without another word, Bubby promptly walked over to the sink, dropped the egg down the garburator and turned it on. Bubby knew I was doing something wrong and because it was Bubby, I felt nothing but more love for her.

Another time, the family went on an outing with Bubby to an outdoor restaurant on a beautiful sunny day. The midday sun cast a shadow across the centre of the table so that some seats were in the hot sun and others in the shade. All eight children were with us and began to argue about who would sit where. Linda and I were unable to control the mayhem. Suddenly and with great calm, Bubby said, "Jack, you sit here. Aaron, you sit there. Jeremy, you sit there," and so on. All of a sudden, the arguing stopped and without a word, each grandchild took his or her assigned seat. When Bubby spoke, you listened. Not out of fear, not because she would shout, but because you knew that Bubby loved you so strongly and respected you so much that you could only love and respect her in return.

Michael's honouring and respect for life, his philosophy of never giving in to age or another's expectations, his strong work ethic and nurturing nature, all guide and inspire his beloved family and numerous wonderful friends to respond, in kind, with honouring and admiration.

— Linda Frimer

Sundown

Sunlight Streaming
(image on page 130)

Photo by Linda Frimer

Biography

Born and raised in Toronto, Michael Frimer attended medical school at the University of Toronto before accepting an internship in general surgery at Vancouver General Hospital, where he became the youngest surgeon in Canada at the time, at age twenty-nine. He continued his surgical practice at Richmond General Hospital.

Frimer is an award-winning darkroom and large-format photographer, with an avid curiosity and desire to tell stories through the process of creativity, often using his images to explore moments captured in time and to observe life as a series of overlapping dimensions that one must look beyond to see life's bigger picture.

He was a proud member of the University of Toronto choir and the Vancouver Cantata Singers. A respected surgeon for over fifty years, Frimer retired from practice in 2018.